LOW-CARB
SNACKS & APPETIZERS

Mid-Morning Munch

Mexican Roll-Ups

6 uncooked lasagna noodles
¾ cup prepared guacamole
¾ cup chunky salsa
¾ cup (3 ounces) shredded fat-free Cheddar cheese
Additional salsa (optional)

1. Cook lasagna noodles according to package directions, omitting salt. Rinse with cool water; drain. Cool.

2. Spread 2 tablespoons guacamole onto each noodle; top each with 2 tablespoons salsa and 2 tablespoons cheese.

3. Roll up noodles jelly-roll fashion. Cut each roll-up in half to form two equal-size roll-ups. Serve immediately with salsa or cover with plastic wrap and refrigerate up to 3 hours. *Makes 12 appetizers*

Health Note: Ten percent of the sodium in American diets comes from natural foods, 75 percent comes from processed and canned goods, and the remaining 15 percent is added during cooking or at the table.

Nutrients per Serving: Calories: 40, Carbohydrate: 4g, Fiber: 1g, Protein: 3g, Fat: 1g, Saturated Fat: 0g, Cholesterol: 2mg, Sodium: 218mg

Mexican Roll-Ups

Hummus-Stuffed Vegetables

1 can (15 ounces) chick-peas, rinsed and drained
1 medium clove garlic
1 tablespoon lemon juice
1 tablespoon olive oil
½ teaspoon ground cumin
¼ teaspoon salt
¼ teaspoon black pepper
1 cup Chinese pea pods (about 24)
¾ pound medium fresh mushrooms (about 24)

1. Combine chick-peas, garlic, lemon juice, oil, cumin, salt and pepper in food processor. Process until smooth. Transfer to piping bag fitted with fluted tip.

2. Remove strings from pea pods. (Some pea pods will not have a stringy portion.) Carefully split pea pods with tip of paring knife. Remove stems from mushrooms; discard.

3. Pipe bean mixture into pea pods and into cavities of inverted mushrooms. Store loosely covered in refrigerator until ready to serve. Garnish just before serving, if desired.   *Makes 12 servings*

Variation: Substitute cucumber slices or red or green bell peppers, cut into 1½-inch triangles, for pea pods and mushrooms.

Nutrients per Serving: Calories: 56, Carbohydrate: 8g, Fiber: 2g, Protein: 3g, Fat: 2g, Saturated Fat: <1g, Cholesterol: 0mg, Sodium: 187mg

Hummus-Stuffed Vegetables

Potato Pancake Appetizers

    3 medium Colorado russet potatoes, peeled and grated
    1 egg
    2 tablespoons all-purpose flour
    1 teaspoon salt
    ¼ teaspoon black pepper
    1 cup grated carrot (1 large)
 1½ cups grated zucchini (2 small)
    ½ cup low-fat sour cream or plain yogurt
    2 tablespoons finely chopped fresh basil
    1 tablespoon chopped chives *or* 1½ teaspoons chili powder

Preheat oven to 425°F. Wrap potatoes in several layers of paper towels; squeeze to remove excess moisture. Beat egg, flour, salt and pepper in large bowl. Add potatoes, carrot and zucchini; mix well. Oil 2 nonstick baking sheets. Place vegetable mixture by heaping spoonfuls onto baking sheets; flatten slightly. Bake 8 to 15 minutes until bottoms are browned. Turn; bake 5 to 10 minutes more. Stir together sour cream and herbs; serve with warm pancakes.

Makes about 24 appetizer pancakes

Favorite recipe from **Colorado Potato Administrative Committee**

Nutrients per Serving: Calories: 30, Carbohydrate: 5g, Fiber: 1g, Protein: 1g, Fat: 1g, Saturated Fat:<1 g, Cholesterol: 11mg, Sodium: 106mg

Peaches and Creamy Dip with Waffle Wedges

    4 ounces reduced-fat cream cheese
    ⅓ cup sugar-free peach preserves
    1 tablespoon fat-free (skim) milk
    2 packages sugar substitute
    ½ teaspoon vanilla
    4 low-fat toaster waffles
      Ground cinnamon to taste

1. Place all ingredients, except waffles and cinnamon, in blender and process until smooth. Set aside.

2. Toast waffles and cut each waffle into 6 wedges.

6

3. Place cream cheese mixture in small serving bowl and sprinkle with cinnamon. Serve with waffle wedges for dipping.

Makes 24 wedges and about ¾ cup cream cheese mixture

Nutrients per Serving: Calories: 54, Carbohydrate: 5g, Fiber: <1g, Protein: 2g, Fat: 3g, Saturated Fat:<1 g, Cholesterol: <1mg, Sodium: 57mg

Pineapple-Mango Salsa

1½ cups DOLE® Fresh Pineapple Chunks
1 ripe DOLE® Mango, peeled and chopped
½ cup chopped red cabbage
⅓ cup finely chopped DOLE® Red Onion
¼ cup chopped fresh cilantro
2 tablespoons lime juice
1 to 2 serrano or jalapeño chiles, seeded and minced

• Stir together pineapple chunks, mango, cabbage, red onion, cilantro, lime juice and chiles in medium bowl. Cover and chill for at least 30 minutes to blend flavors. Serve salsa over grilled chicken with grilled vegetables. Garnish with lime wedges, if desired.

• Salsa can also be served as a dip with tortilla chips or spooned over quesadillas or tacos.

Makes 3½ cups

Prep Time: 15 minutes
Chill Time: 30 minutes

Nutrients per Serving: Calories: 10, Carbohydrate: 3g, Fiber: <1g, Protein: <1g, Fat: <1g, Saturated Fat:0 g, Cholesterol: 0mg, Sodium: <1mg

Cheddar Cheese and Rice Roll

2 cups cooked UNCLE BEN'S® ORIGINAL CONVERTED® Brand Rice
3 cups grated low-fat Cheddar cheese
¾ cup fat-free cream cheese, softened
1 can (4½ ounces) green chilies, drained, chopped
⅛ teaspoon hot sauce
1½ cups chopped walnuts

PREP: CLEAN: Wash hands. Combine rice, Cheddar cheese, cream cheese, chilies and hot sauce. Mix by hand or in food processor. Shape mixture into a log. Roll in walnuts. Wrap tightly with plastic wrap and refrigerate 1 hour.

SERVE: Serve with assorted crackers.

CHILL: Refrigerate leftovers immediately.   *Makes 15 servings*

PREP TIME: 20 minutes
COOK TIME: none

Nutrients per Serving: Calories: 168, Carbohydrate: 10g, Fiber: 1g, Protein: 11g, Fat: 10g, Saturated Fat: 2g, Cholesterol: 7mg, Sodium: 260mg

Helpful Hint

Walnuts are available in many varieties, but the most familiar is the English walnut. The English walnut shell is ridged, light tan in color and oval in shape. One pound unshelled walnuts equals about 1 cup chopped nut meat.

Cheddar Cheese and Rice Roll

Ham and Cheese "Sushi" Rolls

4 thin slices deli ham (about 4×4 inches)
1 package (8 ounces) cream cheese, softened
1 seedless cucumber, quartered lengthwise and cut into 4-inch
**   lengths**
4 thin slices (about 4×4 inches) American or Cheddar cheese,
**   room temperature**
1 red bell pepper, cut into thin 4-inch-long strips

1. For ham sushi: Pat each ham slice with paper towel to remove excess moisture. Spread each ham slice to edges with 2 tablespoons cream cheese.

2. Pat 1 cucumber quarter with paper towel to remove excess moisture; place at edge of ham slice. Roll tightly. Seal by pressing gently. Roll in plastic wrap; refrigerate. Repeat with remaining three ham slices.

3. For cheese sushi: Spread each cheese slice to edges with 2 tablespoons cream cheese.

4. Place 2 strips red pepper even with one edge of one cheese slice. Roll tightly. Seal by pressing gently. Roll in plastic wrap; refrigerate. Repeat with remaining 3 cheese slices.

5. To serve: Remove plastic wrap from ham and cheese rolls. Cut each roll into 8 (½-inch-wide) pieces. Arrange on plate.   *Makes 8 servings*

Nutrients per Serving: Calories: 145, Carbohydrate: 3g, Fiber: <1g, Protein: 5g, Fat: 13g, Saturated Fat: 12g, Cholesterol: 40mg, Sodium: 263mg

Ham and Cheese "Sushi" Rolls

Spinach-Cheddar Squares

1½ cups EGG BEATERS® Healthy Real Egg Product
¾ cup fat-free (skim) milk
1 tablespoon dried onion flakes
1 tablespoon grated Parmesan cheese
¼ teaspoon garlic powder
⅛ teaspoon ground black pepper
¼ cup plain dry bread crumbs
¾ cup shredded fat-free Cheddar cheese, divided
1 (10-ounce) package frozen chopped spinach, thawed and well
  drained
¼ cup diced pimentos

In medium bowl, combine Egg Beaters®, milk, onion flakes, Parmesan cheese, garlic powder and pepper; set aside.

Sprinkle bread crumbs evenly onto bottom of lightly greased 8×8×2-inch baking dish. Top with ½ cup Cheddar cheese and spinach. Pour egg mixture evenly over spinach; top with remaining Cheddar cheese and pimentos.

Bake at 350°F for 35 to 40 minutes or until knife inserted in center comes out clean. Let stand 10 minutes before serving.

Makes 16 appetizer servings

Prep Time: 15 minutes
Cook Time: 40 minutes

Nutrients per Serving: Calories: 37, Carbohydrate: 4g, Fiber: 1g, Protein: 5g, Fat: <1g, Saturated Fat: <1g, Cholesterol: <1mg, Sodium: 116mg

Chicken Nachos

22 (about 1 ounce) GUILTLESS GOURMET® Baked Tortilla Chips
    (yellow, red or blue corn)
½ cup (4 ounces) cooked and shredded boneless chicken breast
¼ cup chopped green onions
¼ cup (1 ounce) shredded Cheddar cheese
    Sliced green and red chilies (optional)

Microwave Directions

Spread tortilla chips on flat microwave-safe plate. Sprinkle chicken, onions and cheese over chips. Microwave on HIGH 30 seconds until cheese starts to bubble. Serve hot. Garnish with chilies, if desired.

Conventional Directions

Preheat oven to 325°F. Spread tortilla chips on baking sheet. Sprinkle chicken, onions and cheese over chips. Bake about 5 minutes or until cheese starts to bubble. Serve hot.   *Makes 22 nachos*

Nutrients per Serving: Calories: 20, Carbohydrate: 1g, Fiber: <1g, Protein: 2g, Fat: 1g, Saturated Fat: <1g, Cholesterol: 6mg, Sodium: 21mg

Monterey Wedges

  2 (6-inch) corn tortillas
  ¼ cup (1 ounce) shredded reduced-fat Monterey Jack or sharp
      Cheddar cheese
  ½ teaspoon chili powder
  ½ cup chopped green bell pepper
  1 plum tomato, chopped (about ¼ cup)
  2 tablespoons chopped canned green chilies
  ¼ cup sliced ripe olives, drained

1. Preheat oven 425°F. Coat nonstick baking sheet with nonstick cooking spray.

2. Place tortillas on baking sheet; top each with 2 tablespoons cheese, half the chili powder, bell pepper, tomato, chilies and olives. Top with remaining 2 tablespoons cheese.

3. Bake 5 minutes or until cheese melts. Remove from oven and let stand on baking sheet 3 minutes for easier handling. Cut into 4 wedges.
                    Makes 4 servings (2 wedges each)

Nutrients per Serving: Calories: 85, Carbohydrate: 8g, Fiber: 1g, Protein: 3g, Fat: 5g, Saturated Fat: 1g, Cholesterol: 5mg, Sodium: 387mg

Turkey-Broccoli Roll-Ups

2 pounds broccoli spears
⅓ cup fat-free sour cream
¼ cup reduced-fat mayonnaise
2 tablespoons thawed frozen orange juice concentrate
1 tablespoon Dijon mustard
1 teaspoon dried basil leaves
1 pound smoked turkey, very thinly sliced

1. Arrange broccoli spears in single layer in large, shallow microwavable dish. Add 1 tablespoon water. Cover dish tightly with plastic wrap; vent. Microwave at HIGH (100%) 6 to 7 minutes or just until broccoli is crisp-tender, rearranging spears after 4 minutes. Carefully remove plastic wrap; drain broccoli. Immediately place broccoli in cold water to stop cooking; drain well. Pat dry with paper towels.

2. Combine sour cream, mayonnaise, juice concentrate, mustard and basil in small bowl; mix well.

3. Cut turkey slices into 2-inch-wide strips. Spread sour cream mixture evenly on strips. Place 1 broccoli piece at short end of each strip. Starting at short end, roll up tightly (allow broccoli spear to protrude from one end). Place on serving platter; cover with plastic wrap. Refrigerate until ready to serve. Garnish just before serving, if desired.

Makes 20 servings

Note: To blanch broccoli on stove top, bring small amount of water to a boil in saucepan. Add broccoli spears; cover. Simmer 2 to 3 minutes or until broccoli is crisp-tender; drain. Cool; continue as directed.

Nutrients per Serving: Calories: 51, Carbohydrate: 4g, Fiber: 2g, Protein: 7g, Fat: 1g, Saturated Fat: <1g, Cholesterol: 10mg, Sodium: 259mg

Turkey-Broccoli Roll-Ups

Angelic Deviled Eggs

6 eggs
¼ cup low-fat (1%) cottage cheese
3 tablespoons prepared fat-free ranch dressing
2 teaspoons Dijon mustard
2 tablespoons minced fresh chives or dill
1 tablespoon diced well-drained pimiento or roasted red pepper

1. Place eggs in medium saucepan; add enough water to cover. Bring to a boil over medium heat. Remove from heat; cover. Let stand 15 minutes. Drain. Add cold water to eggs in saucepan; let stand until eggs are cool. Drain. Remove shells from eggs.

2. Cut eggs lengthwise in half. Remove yolks, reserving 3 yolk halves. Discard remaining yolks or reserve for another use. Place egg whites, cut sides up, on serving plate; cover with plastic wrap. Refrigerate while preparing filling.

3. Combine cottage cheese, dressing, mustard and reserved yolk halves in mini food processor; process until smooth. (Or, place in small bowl and mash with fork until well blended.) Transfer cheese mixture to small bowl; stir in chives and pimiento. Spoon into egg whites. Cover and chill at least 1 hour. Garnish, if desired.   *Makes 12 servings*

Nutrients per Serving: Calories: 24, Carbohydrate: 1g, Fiber: 1g, Protein: 3g, Fat: 1g, Saturated Fat: <1g, Cholesterol: 27mg, Sodium: 96mg

Angelic Deviled Eggs

Afternoon Snack

Finger Lickin' Chicken Salad

½ cup purchased carved roasted skinless chicken breast
½ rib celery, cut into 1-inch pieces
¼ cup drained mandarin orange segments
¼ cup red seedless grapes
2 tablespoons fat-free sugar-free lemon yogurt
1 tablespoon reduced-fat mayonnaise
¼ teaspoon reduced-sodium soy sauce
⅛ teaspoon pumpkin pie spice or cinnamon

1. Toss together chicken, celery, oranges and grapes. Place in covered plastic container.

2. For dipping sauce, stir together yogurt, mayonnaise, soy sauce and pumpkin pie spice.

3. Pack chicken mixture and dipping sauce in insulated bag with ice pack. To serve, dip chicken mixture into dipping sauce.

Makes 1 serving

Variation: Alternately thread the chicken, celery, oranges and grapes on wooden skewers for a creative variation to this recipe.

Nutrients per Serving: Calories: 207, Carbohydrate: 15g, Fiber: 1g, Protein: 24g, Fat: 6g, Saturated Fat: 1g, Cholesterol: 64mg, Sodium: 212mg

Finger Lickin' Chicken Salad

Confetti Tuna in Celery Sticks

**1 (3-ounce) pouch of STARKIST® Premium Albacore
or Chunk Light Tuna**
½ cup shredded red or green cabbage
½ cup shredded carrot
¼ cup shredded yellow squash or zucchini
3 tablespoons reduced-calorie cream cheese, softened
1 tablespoon plain low-fat yogurt
½ teaspoon dried basil, crushed
Salt and pepper to taste
10 to 12 (4-inch) celery sticks, with leaves if desired

1. In a small bowl toss together tuna, cabbage, carrot and squash.

2. Stir in cream cheese, yogurt and basil. Add salt and pepper to taste.

3. With small spatula spread mixture evenly into celery sticks.

Makes 10 to 12 servings

Prep Time: 20 minutes

Nutrients per Serving: Calories: 32, Carbohydrate: 3g, Fiber: 1g,
Protein: 3g, Fat: 1g, Saturated Fat: 1g, Cholesterol: 5mg, Sodium: 90mg

Cheesy Chips

10 wonton wrappers
**2 tablespoons powdered American cheese
or grated Parmesan cheese**
2 teaspoons olive oil
⅛ teaspoon garlic powder

1. Preheat oven to 375°F. Spray baking sheet with nonstick cooking spray.

2. Diagonally cut each wonton wrapper in half, forming two triangles.
Place in single layer on prepared baking sheet.

3. Combine cheese, oil and garlic powder in small bowl. Sprinkle over
wonton triangles.

4. Bake 6 to 8 minutes or until golden brown and crisp. Remove from
oven. Cool completely. *Makes 4 servings*

Nutrients per Serving: Calories: 75, Carbohydrate: 9g, Fiber: <1g,
Protein: 2g, Fat: 3g, Saturated Fat: 1g, Cholesterol: 4mg, Sodium: 92mg

Confetti Tuna in Celery Sticks

Herbed Potato Chips

Nonstick olive oil cooking spray
2 medium red potatoes (about ½ pound), unpeeled
1 tablespoon olive oil
2 tablespoons minced fresh dill, thyme or rosemary *or*
   2 teaspoons dried dill weed, thyme or rosemary
¼ teaspoon garlic salt
⅛ teaspoon black pepper
1¼ cups fat-free sour cream

1. Preheat oven to 450°F. Spray large baking sheets with cooking spray; set aside.

2. Cut potatoes crosswise into very thin slices, about ¹⁄₁₆ inch thick. Pat dry with paper towels. Arrange potato slices in single layer on prepared baking sheets; coat potatoes with cooking spray.

3. Bake 10 minutes; turn slices over. Brush with oil. Combine dill, garlic salt and pepper in small bowl; sprinkle evenly onto potato slices. Continue baking 5 to 10 minutes or until potatoes are golden brown. Cool on baking sheets.

4. Serve with sour cream.   *Makes 6 servings (about 60 chips)*

Nutrients per Serving: Calories: 76, Carbohydrate: 9g, Fiber: <1g, Protein: 6g, Fat: 2g, Saturated Fat: <1g, Cholesterol: 0mg, Sodium: 113mg

Helpful Hint

Always choose firm, relatively smooth, clean potatoes. Potatoes should be reasonably well-shaped and free from cuts or bruises. Avoid green-colored potatoes and those with sprouts. When cooking potatoes, leave skins on when possible; they add extra nutrition and good taste.

Herbed Potato Chips

Mini Marinated Beef Skewers

1 beef top round steak (about 1 pound)
2 tablespoons reduced-sodium soy sauce
1 tablespoon dry sherry
1 teaspoon dark sesame oil
2 cloves garlic, minced
18 cherry tomatoes (optional)

1. Cut beef crosswise into ⅛-inch slices. Place in large resealable plastic food storage bag. Combine soy sauce, sherry, oil and garlic in cup; pour over steak. Seal bag; turn to coat. Marinate in refrigerator at least 30 minutes or up to 2 hours.

2. Soak 18 (6-inch) skewers in water 20 minutes.

3. Drain steak; discard marinade. Weave beef accordion-style onto skewers. Place on rack of broiler pan.

4. Broil 4 to 5 inches from heat 2 minutes. Turn skewers over; broil 2 minutes or until beef is barely pink.

5. If desired, garnish each skewer with 1 cherry tomato. Place skewers on lettuce-lined platter. Serve warm.

Makes 6 servings (3 skewers each)

Nutrients per Serving: Calories: 120, Carbohydrate: 2g, Fiber: <1g, Protein: 20g, Fat: 4g, Saturated Fat: 1g, Cholesterol: 60mg, Sodium: 99mg

Mini Marinated Beef Skewers

Portobello Mushrooms Sesame

4 large portobello mushrooms
2 tablespoons sweet rice wine
2 tablespoons reduced-sodium soy sauce
2 cloves garlic, minced
1 teaspoon dark sesame oil

1. Remove and discard stems from mushrooms; set caps aside. Combine remaining ingredients in small bowl.

2. Brush both sides of mushrooms with soy sauce mixture. Grill mushrooms top side up on covered grill over medium coals 3 to 4 minutes. Brush tops with soy sauce mixture and turn over; grill 2 minutes more or until mushrooms are lightly browned. Turn again and grill, basting frequently, 4 to 5 minutes or until tender when pressed with back of spatula. Remove mushrooms and cut diagonally into ½-inch-thick slices. *Makes 4 servings*

Nutrients per Serving: Calories: 67, Carbohydrate: 9g, Fiber: <1g, Protein: 4g, Fat: 2g, Saturated Fat: <1g, Cholesterol: 0mg, Sodium: 268mg

Herbed-Stuffed Tomatoes

15 cherry tomatoes
½ cup 1% low-fat cottage cheese
1 tablespoon thinly sliced green onion
1 teaspoon chopped fresh chervil *or* ¼ teaspoon dried chervil leaves
½ teaspoon snipped fresh dill *or* ⅛ teaspoon dried dill weed
⅛ teaspoon lemon pepper

Cut thin slice off bottom of each tomato. Scoop out pulp with small spoon; discard pulp. Invert tomatoes onto paper towels to drain.

Combine cottage cheese, green onion, chervil, dill and lemon pepper in small bowl. Spoon into tomatoes. Serve immediately, or cover and refrigerate up to 8 hours. *Makes 5 servings*

Nutrients per Serving: Calories: 27, Carbohydrate: 3g, Fiber: <1g, Protein: 3g, Fat: <1g, Saturated Fat: <1g, Cholesterol: 1mg, Sodium: 96mg

Portobello Mushrooms Sesame

Far East Tabbouleh

¾ **cup uncooked bulgur**
1¾ **cups boiling water**
2 **tablespoons reduced-sodium teriyaki sauce**
2 **tablespoons lemon juice**
1 **tablespoon olive oil**
¾ **cup diced seeded cucumber**
¾ **cup diced seeded tomato**
½ **cup thinly sliced green onions**
½ **cup minced fresh cilantro or parsley**
1 **tablespoon minced fresh ginger**
1 **clove garlic, minced**

1. Combine bulgur and water in small bowl. Cover with plastic wrap; let stand 45 minutes or until bulgur is puffed, stirring occasionally. Drain in wire mesh sieve; discard liquid.

2. Combine bulgur, teriyaki sauce, lemon juice and oil in large bowl. Stir in cucumber, tomato, onions, cilantro, ginger and garlic until well blended. Cover; refrigerate 4 hours, stirring occasionally. Garnish as desired.   *Makes 4 servings*

Health Note: When it comes to reducing the total fat in your diet, it is often the small changes that have the greatest effect. For instance, substituting 1 ounce of pretzels for 1 ounce of potato chips eliminates more than 9 grams of fat.

Nutrients per Serving: Calories: 73, Carbohydrate: 13g, Fiber: 3g, Protein: 2g, Fat: 2g, Saturated Fat: <1g, Cholesterol: 0mg, Sodium: 156mg

Far East Tabbouleh

Mini Vegetable Quiches

2 cups cut-up vegetables (bell peppers, broccoli, zucchini and/or
    carrots)
2 tablespoons chopped green onions
2 tablespoons FLEISCHMANN'S® Original Margarine
4 (8-inch) flour tortillas, each cut into 8 triangles
1 cup EGG BEATERS® Healthy Real Egg Product
1 cup fat-free (skim) milk
½ teaspoon dried basil leaves

In medium nonstick skillet, over medium-high heat, sauté vegetables
and green onions in margarine until tender.

Arrange 4 tortilla pieces in each of 8 (6-ounce) greased custard cups or
ramekins, placing points of tortilla pieces at center of bottom of each
cup and pressing lightly to form shape of cup. Divide vegetable mixture
evenly among cups. In small bowl, combine Egg Beaters®, milk and basil.
Pour evenly over vegetable mixture. Place cups on baking sheet. Bake at
375°F for 20 to 25 minutes or until puffed and knife inserted into
centers comes out clean. Let stand 5 minutes before serving.

Makes 8 servings

Nutrients per Serving: Calories: 115, Carbohydrate: 14g, Fiber: 1g,
Protein: 6g, Fat: 4g, Saturated Fat: 1g, Cholesterol: 1mg,
Sodium: 184mg

Mini Vegetable Quiches

Pinwheel Appetizers

3 cups cooked wild rice
1 package (8 ounces) nonfat pasteurized process cream cheese
    product
⅓ cup grated Parmesan cheese
1 teaspoon dried parsley flakes
½ teaspoon garlic powder
½ teaspoon Dijon-style mustard
2 to 3 drops hot pepper sauce (optional)
3 (12-inch) soft flour tortillas
2½ ounces thinly sliced corned beef
9 fresh spinach leaves

Combine wild rice, cream cheese, Parmesan cheese, parsley, garlic powder, mustard and pepper sauce. Spread evenly over tortillas, leaving ½-inch border on one side of each tortilla. Place single layer corned beef over rice and cheese mixture. Top with layer of spinach. Roll each tortilla tightly toward ½-inch border. Moisten border of tortilla with water; press to seal roll. Wrap tightly in plastic wrap. Refrigerate several hours or overnight. Cut into 1-inch slices.   *Makes 36 appetizers*

Favorite recipe from **Minnesota Cultivated Wild Rice Council**

Nutrients per Serving: Calories: 37, Carbohydrate: 5g, Fiber: <1g, Protein: 2g, Fat: 1g, Saturated Fat: <1g, Cholesterol: 4mg, Sodium: 91mg

Helpful Hint

To make 3 cups of wild rice, bring 2½ cups water to a boil in a medium saucepan over medium-high heat. Add 1 cup rinsed and drained wild rice and ½ teaspoon salt. Return water to a boil. Reduce heat to low. Cover and cook for 40 to 45 minutes until all the water is absorbed and the rice is tender.

Pinwheel Appetizers

Oriental Chicken Balls

1 tablespoon butter or margarine
1 tablespoon all-purpose flour
½ cup warm milk
3 tablespoons finely chopped onion
1 cup chopped cooked chicken
1 teaspoon lemon juice
1 tablespoon chopped fresh parsley
½ teaspoon salt
⅛ teaspoon ground black pepper
⅓ cup cornstarch
  Vegetable oil for frying
  Sweet and sour sauce

Melt butter in small skillet over medium heat until hot; stir in flour and cook until smooth and lightly browned. Slowly stir in milk until sauce is thick and smooth. Bring to a boil, stirring constantly. Stir in onion; cook about 5 minutes over low heat. Stir in chicken, lemon juice, parsley, salt and pepper; transfer to small bowl. Refrigerate until cold. Shape into 1-inch balls; keep refrigerated until ready to cook. Place cornstarch on wax paper. Roll chicken balls in cornstarch. Heat 1 inch oil in large skillet to 375°F. Add chicken balls; cook only until light brown. Serve hot with sweet and sour sauce for dipping.

Makes 10 servings (about 30 to 34 appetizers)

Favorite recipe from **National Chicken Council**

Nutrients per Serving: Calories: 201, Carbohydrate: 10g, Fiber: 0g, Protein: 4g, Fat: 16g, Saturated Fat: 3g, Cholesterol: 16mg, Sodium: 166mg

Stuffed Portobello Mushrooms

4 portobello mushrooms (4 ounces each)
¼ cup olive oil
2 cloves garlic, pressed
6 ounces crumbled goat cheese
2 ounces prosciutto or thinly sliced ham, chopped
¼ cup chopped fresh basil
  Mixed salad greens

Remove stems and gently scrape gills from underside of mushrooms; discard stems and gills. Brush mushroom caps with combined oil and garlic. Combine cheese, prosciutto and basil in medium bowl. Grill mushrooms, top side up, on covered grill over medium KINGSFORD® Briquets 4 minutes. Turn mushrooms over; fill caps with cheese mixture, dividing equally. Cover and grill 3 to 4 minutes longer until cheese mixture is warm. Remove mushrooms from grill; cut into quarters. Serve on mixed greens. *Makes 4 servings*

Nutrients per Serving: Calories: 298, Carbohydrate: 8g, Fiber: 0g, Protein: 13g, Fat: 25g, Saturated Fat: 0g, Cholesterol: 28mg, Sodium: 353mg

Mini Burgers

   1 pound ground chicken
   ¼ cup Italian-style dry bread crumbs
   ¼ cup chili sauce
   1 egg white
   1 tablespoon white Worcestershire sauce
   2 teaspoons Dijon-style mustard
   ½ teaspoon dried thyme leaves
   ¼ teaspoon garlic powder
   32 thin slices plum tomatoes (about 3 medium)
   ½ cup sweet onion slices (about 1 small)
   16 slices cocktail rye or pumpernickel bread
      Mustard (optional)
      Pickle slices (optional)
      Snipped chives or green onion tops (optional)

1. Preheat oven to 350°F. Combine chicken, bread crumbs, chili sauce, egg white, Worcestershire sauce, mustard, thyme and garlic powder in medium bowl. Form mixture into 16 patties.

2. Place patties in 15×10-inch jelly-roll pan. Bake, uncovered, 10 to 15 minutes or until patties are no longer pink in centers.

3. Place 2 tomato slices and 1 onion slice on each bread slice. Top each with 1 patty; add dollops of mustard, pickle slices and chives, if desired.
Makes 16 servings

Nutrients per Serving: Calories: 74, Carbohydrate: 7g, Fiber: 1g, Protein: 6g, Fat: 2g, Saturated Fat: 1g, Cholesterol: 14mg, Sodium: 149mg

Party Appetizers

Buffalo Chicken Tenders

3 tablespoons Louisiana-style hot sauce
½ teaspoon paprika
¼ teaspoon ground red pepper
1 pound chicken tenders
½ cup fat-free blue cheese dressing
¼ cup reduced-fat sour cream
2 tablespoons crumbled blue cheese
1 medium red bell pepper, cut into ½-inch slices

1. Preheat oven to 375°F. Combine hot sauce, paprika and ground red pepper in small bowl; brush on all surfaces of chicken. Place chicken in greased 11×7-inch baking dish. Cover; marinate in refrigerator 30 minutes.

2. Bake, uncovered, about 15 minutes or until chicken is no longer pink in center.

3. Combine blue cheese dressing, sour cream and blue cheese in small serving bowl. Garnish as desired. Serve with chicken and bell pepper for dipping. *Makes 10 servings*

Nutrients per Serving: Calories: 83, Carbohydrate: 5g, Fiber: 0g, Protein: 9g, Fat: 2g, Saturated Fat: 1g, Cholesterol: 27mg, Sodium: 180mg

Buffalo Chicken Tenders

Southern Crab Cakes with Rémoulade Dipping Sauce

  10 ounces fresh lump crabmeat
1½ cups fresh white or sourdough bread crumbs, divided
  ¼ cup chopped green onions
  ½ cup fat-free or reduced-fat mayonnaise, divided
  1 egg white, lightly beaten
  2 tablespoons coarse grain or spicy brown mustard, divided
  ¾ teaspoon hot pepper sauce, divided
  2 teaspoons olive oil, divided
     Lemon wedges

1. Preheat oven to 200°F. Combine crabmeat, ¾ cup bread crumbs and green onions in medium bowl. Add ¼ cup mayonnaise, egg white, 1 tablespoon mustard and ½ teaspoon pepper sauce; mix well. Using ¼ cup mixture per cake, shape eight ½-inch-thick cakes. Roll crab cakes lightly in remaining ¾ cup bread crumbs.

2. Heat large nonstick skillet over medium heat until hot; add 1 teaspoon oil. Add 4 crab cakes; cook 4 to 5 minutes per side or until golden brown. Transfer to serving platter; keep warm in oven. Repeat with remaining 1 teaspoon oil and crab cakes.

3. To prepare dipping sauce, combine remaining ¼ cup mayonnaise, 1 tablespoon mustard and ¼ teaspoon hot pepper sauce in small bowl; mix well.

4. Serve crab cakes warm with lemon wedges and dipping sauce.

Makes 8 servings

Nutrients per Serving: Calories: 81, Carbohydrate: 8g, Fiber: <1g, Protein: 7g, Fat: 2g, Saturated Fat: <1g, Cholesterol: 30mg, Sodium: 376mg

Southern Crab Cakes with Rémoulade Dipping Sauce

Spicy Orange Chicken Kabob Appetizers

2 boneless skinless chicken breasts
1 small red or green bell pepper
24 small fresh button mushrooms
½ cup orange juice
2 tablespoons reduced-sodium soy sauce
1 tablespoon vegetable oil
1½ teaspoons onion powder
½ teaspoon Chinese five-spice powder

1. Cut chicken and pepper each into 24 (¾-inch) square pieces. Place chicken, pepper and mushrooms in large resealable plastic food storage bag. Combine juice, soy sauce, oil, onion powder and five-spice powder in small bowl. Pour over chicken mixture. Close bag securely; turn to coat. Marinate in refrigerator 4 to 24 hours, turning frequently.

2. Soak 24 small wooden skewers or toothpicks in water 20 minutes. Meanwhile, preheat broiler. Coat broiler pan with nonstick cooking spray.

3. Drain chicken, pepper and mushrooms, reserving marinade. Thread 1 piece chicken, 1 piece pepper and 1 mushroom onto each skewer. Place on prepared pan. Brush with marinade; discard remaining marinade. Broil 4 inches from heat source 5 to 6 minutes until chicken is no longer pink in center. Serve immediately.   *Makes 12 servings*

Nutrients per Serving: Calories: 30, Carbohydrate: 2g, Fiber: <1g, Protein: 4g, Fat: <1g, Saturated Fat: <1g, Cholesterol: 10mg, Sodium: 38mg

Spicy Orange Chicken Kabob Appetizers

Jicama & Shrimp Cocktail with Roasted Red Pepper Sauce

2 large red bell peppers
6 ounces (about 24 medium-large) shrimp, peeled and deveined
1 medium clove garlic
1½ cups fresh cilantro sprigs
2 tablespoons lime juice
2 tablespoons orange juice
½ teaspoon hot pepper sauce
1 small jicama (about ¾ pound), peeled and cut into strips
1 plum tomato, halved, seeded and thinly sliced

1. Place bell peppers on broiler pan. Broil, 4 to 6 inches from heat, about 6 minutes, turning every 2 to 3 minutes or until all sides are charred. Transfer peppers to paper bag; close bag tightly. Let stand 10 minutes or until peppers are cool enough to handle and skins are loosened. Peel peppers; cut in half. Remove cores, seeds and membranes; discard.

2. Add shrimp to large saucepan of boiling water. Reduce heat to medium-low; simmer, uncovered, 2 to 3 minutes or until shrimp turn pink. Drain shrimp; rinse under cold running water. Cover; refrigerate until ready to use.

3. Place peppers and garlic in food processor; process until peppers are coarsely chopped. Add cilantro, lime juice, orange juice and pepper sauce; process until cilantro is finely chopped but mixture is not puréed.

4. Combine jicama, shrimp and tomato in large bowl. Add bell pepper mixture; toss to coat evenly. Serve over lettuce. *Makes 8 servings*

Nutrients per Serving: Calories: 69, Carbohydrate: 10g, Fiber: 1g, Protein: 6g, Fat: 1g, Saturated Fat: <1g, Cholesterol: 42mg, Sodium: 120mg

Jicama & Shrimp Cocktail with Roasted Red Pepper Sauce

Carpaccio di Zucchini

¾ **pound zucchini, shredded**
½ **cup sliced almonds, toasted**
1 **tablespoon prepared Italian dressing**
4 **French bread baguettes, sliced in half lengthwise**
4 **teaspoons soft spread margarine**
3 **tablespoons grated Parmesan cheese**

1. Preheat broiler. Place zucchini in medium bowl. Add almonds and dressing; mix well. Set aside.

2. Place baguette halves on large baking sheet; spread evenly with margarine. Sprinkle with cheese. Broil 3 inches from heat 2 to 3 minutes or until edges and cheese are browned.

3. Spread zucchini mixture evenly on each baguette half. Serve immediately.

Makes 4 servings

Go-with suggestions: Spaghetti with tomato sauce.

Prep and Cook Time: 28 minutes

Nutrients per Serving: Calories: 180, Carbohydrate: 6g, Fiber: 2g, Protein: 6g, Fat: 15g, Saturated Fat: 0g, Cholesterol: 4mg, Sodium: 305mg

Helpful Hint

Zucchini are available all year with their peak season from July to September.

Carpaccio di Zucchini

Eggplant Caviar

1 large eggplant, unpeeled
¼ cup chopped onion
2 tablespoons lemon juice
1 tablespoon olive or vegetable oil
1 small clove garlic
½ teaspoon salt
½ teaspoon TABASCO® brand Pepper Sauce
  Sieved hard-cooked egg white (optional)
  Lemon slices (optional)

Preheat oven to 350°F. Place eggplant in shallow baking dish. Bake
1 hour or until soft, turning once. Trim off ends; slice eggplant in half
lengthwise. Place cut-side-down in colander and let drain 10 minutes.
Scoop out pulp; reserve pulp and peel. Combine eggplant peel, onion,
lemon juice, oil, garlic, salt and TABASCO® Sauce in blender or food
processor. Cover and process until peel is finely chopped. Add eggplant
pulp. Cover and process just until chopped. Place in serving dish.
Garnish with egg white and lemon slices, if desired. Serve with toast
points, if desired.   *Makes 1½ cups*

Nutrients per Serving: Calories: 10, Carbohydrate: 2g, Fiber: 1g,
Protein: <1g, Fat: 1g, Saturated Fat: <1g, Cholesterol: 0mg,
Sodium: 45mg

Spicy Deviled Eggs

6 eggs
3 tablespoons heavy cream
1 green onion, finely chopped
1 tablespoon white wine vinegar
2 teaspoons Dijon mustard
½ teaspoon curry powder
½ teaspoon hot pepper sauce
3 tablespoons crisply cooked chopped bacon
1 tablespoon chopped fresh chives or parsley, for garnish

1. Place eggs into small saucepan; cover with cold water. Bring to a boil
over high heat. Cover and remove from heat. Let stand 15 minutes.
Drain; rinse under cold water. Peel eggs; cool completely.

2. Slice eggs in half lengthwise. Remove yolks to small bowl; set whites aside. Mash yolks with fork. Stir in cream, onion, vinegar, mustard, curry powder and pepper sauce until blended.

3. Spoon or pipe egg yolk mixture into centers of egg whites. Arrange eggs on serving plate. Garnish eggs with bacon and chives.

Makes 12 deviled eggs

Nutrients per Serving: Calories: 89, Carbohydrate: <1g, Fiber: <1g, Protein: 6g, Fat: 6g, Saturated Fat: 2g, Cholesterol: 218mg, Sodium: 85mg

Blue Crab Stuffed Tomatoes

 ½ **pound Florida blue crabmeat**
 10 **plum tomatoes**
 ½ **cup finely chopped celery**
 ⅓ **cup plain low fat yogurt**
 2 **tablespoons minced green onion**
 2 **tablespoons finely chopped red bell pepper**
 ½ **teaspoon lemon juice**
 ¼ **teaspoon salt**
 ⅛ **teaspoon black pepper**

Remove any shell or cartilage from crabmeat.

Cut tomatoes in half lengthwise. Carefully scoop out centers of tomatoes; discard pulp. Invert on paper towels.

Combine crabmeat, celery, yogurt, onion, red pepper, lemon juice, salt and black pepper. Mix well.

Fill tomato halves with crab mixture. Refrigerate 2 hours.

Makes 20 appetizers

Favorite recipe from **Florida Department of Agriculture and Consumer Services, Bureau of Seafood and Aquaculture**

Nutrients per Serving: Calories: 46, Carbohydrate: 3g, Fiber: 1g, Protein: 7g, Fat: 1g, Saturated Fat: <1g, Cholesterol: 27mg, Sodium: 138mg

Jerk Wings with Ranch Dipping Sauce

½ cup mayonnaise
½ cup plain yogurt or sour cream
1½ teaspoons salt, divided
1¼ teaspoons garlic powder, divided
½ teaspoon black pepper, divided
¼ teaspoon onion powder
2 tablespoons orange juice
1 teaspoon sugar
1 teaspoon dried thyme leaves
1 teaspoon paprika
¼ teaspoon ground nutmeg
¼ teaspoon ground red pepper
2½ pounds chicken wings (about 10 wings)

1. Preheat oven to 450°F. For Ranch Dipping Sauce, combine mayonnaise, yogurt, ½ teaspoon salt, ¼ teaspoon garlic powder, ¼ teaspoon black pepper and onion powder in small bowl.

2. Combine orange juice, sugar, thyme, paprika, nutmeg, red pepper, remaining 1 teaspoon salt, 1 teaspoon garlic powder and ¼ teaspoon black pepper in small bowl.

3. Cut tips from wings; discard. Place wings in large bowl. Drizzle with orange juice mixture; toss to coat.

4. Transfer chicken to greased broiler pan. Bake 25 to 30 minutes or until juices run clear and skin is crisp. Serve with Ranch Dipping Sauce.

Makes 6 to 7 servings

Serving Suggestion: Serve with celery sticks.

Nutrients per Serving: Calories: 363, Carbohydrate: 4g, Fiber: <1g, Protein: 20g, Fat: 30g, Saturated Fat: 12g, Cholesterol: 69mg, Sodium: 699mg

Jerk Wings with Ranch Dipping Sauce

Smoked Salmon Appetizers

¼ cup reduced-fat or fat-free cream cheese, softened
1 tablespoon chopped fresh dill *or* 1 teaspoon dried dill weed
⅛ teaspoon ground red pepper
4 ounces thinly sliced smoked salmon or lox
24 melba toast rounds or other low-fat crackers

1. Combine cream cheese, dill and pepper in small bowl; stir to blend. Spread evenly over each slice of salmon. Roll up salmon slices jelly-roll fashion. Place on plate; cover with plastic wrap. Chill at least 1 hour or up to 4 hours before serving.

2. Using a sharp knife, cut salmon rolls crosswise into ¾-inch pieces. Place pieces, cut side down, on serving plate. Garnish each salmon roll with dill sprig, if desired. Serve cold or at room temperature with melba rounds. *Makes about 2 dozen appetizers*

Nutrients per Serving: Calories: 80, Carbohydrate: 10g, Fiber: 1g, Protein: 6g, Fat: 2g, Saturated Fat: 1g, Cholesterol: 6mg, Sodium: 241mg

Caponata Spread

1½ tablespoons BERTOLLI® Olive Oil
1 medium eggplant, diced (about 4 cups)
1 medium onion, chopped
1½ cups water
1 envelope LIPTON® RECIPE SECRETS® Savory Herb with Garlic Soup Mix
2 tablespoons chopped fresh parsley (optional)
Salt and ground black pepper to taste
Pita chips or thinly sliced Italian or French bread

In 10-inch nonstick skillet, heat oil over medium heat and cook eggplant with onion 3 minutes. Add ½ cup water. Reduce heat to low and simmer covered 3 minutes. Stir in soup mix blended with remaining 1 cup water. Bring to a boil over high heat. Reduce heat to low and simmer uncovered, stirring occasionally, 20 minutes. Stir in parsley, salt and pepper. Serve with pita chips. *Makes about 4 cups spread*

Nutrients per Serving: Calories: 13, Carbohydrate: 2g, Fiber: <1g, Protein: <1g, Fat: 1g, Saturated Fat: <1g, Cholesterol: 0mg, Sodium: 60mg

Smoked Salmon Appetizers

Chicken Satay

1 pound chicken tenders or boneless skinless chicken breasts, cut into 8 strips
2 tablespoons light soy sauce
Satay Dipping Sauce
  2 tablespoons finely chopped onion
  1 clove garlic, minced
    Dash ground ginger
½ cup regular or reduced-fat chunky peanut butter
  3 to 4 tablespoons light soy sauce
  3 to 4 tablespoons white wine vinegar or rice wine vinegar
  1 teaspoon sugar

1. Place chicken in 8×8-inch baking pan; drizzle with 2 tablespoons soy sauce and toss. Let stand 5 to 10 minutes.

2. Thread 1 chicken tender on metal or bamboo skewer. Repeat with remaining chicken tenders. Arrange skewers on broiler pan. Broil 4 inches from heat 3 to 5 minutes per side or until chicken is no longer pink in center.

3. While chicken is cooking, prepare Satay Dipping Sauce. To prepare sauce, spray small saucepan with nonstick cooking spray; heat over medium heat until hot. Add onion, garlic and ginger; cook and stir 2 to 3 minutes or until onion is tender. Add remaining ingredients; cook 5 minutes, stirring constantly, until smooth and hot. Spoon into bowl for dipping.

4. Arrange chicken on serving platter. Serve with Satay Dipping Sauce.
Makes 8 servings

Prep and Cook Time: 30 minutes

Nutrients per Serving: Calories: 171, Carbohydrate: 5g, Fiber: 1g, Protein: 17g, Fat: 9g, Saturated Fat: 0g, Cholesterol: 34mg, Sodium: 372mg

Best of the Wurst Spread

1 tablespoon butter or margarine
½ cup finely chopped onion
1 package (16 ounces) liverwurst
¼ cup mayonnaise or salad dressing
¼ cup finely chopped dill pickle
2 teaspoons horseradish mustard or spicy brown mustard
1 tablespoon drained capers
2 teaspoons dried dill weed
¼ small dill pickle, cut into strips
   Cocktail rye bread for serving

1. Heat butter in small saucepan over medium heat until melted. Add onion; cook and stir 5 minutes or until tender. Mash liverwurst with fork in medium bowl; beat in onion, mayonnaise, chopped dill pickle, mustard, capers and dill weed.

2. Form liverwurst mixture into football shape on serving plate; decorate with dill pickle strips to look like football laces. Serve with bread.

Makes 12 (3-tablespoon) servings

Serve It With Style!: For added flavor, serve the spread with mustard toast instead of rye bread. To prepare mustard toast, lightly spread horseradish mustard or spicy brown mustard on cocktail rye bread slices. Broil, 4 inches from heat, until lightly browned.

Prep and Cook Time: 15 minutes

Nutrients per Serving: Calories: 168, Carbohydrate: 2g, Fiber: <1g, Protein: 5g, Fat: 16g, Saturated Fat: 0g, Cholesterol: 64mg, Sodium: 128mg

Spiced Sesame Wonton Crisps

20 (3-inch-square) wonton wrappers, cut in half
1 tablespoon water
2 teaspoons olive oil
½ teaspoon paprika
½ teaspoon ground cumin or chili powder
¼ teaspoon dry mustard
1 tablespoon sesame seeds

1. Preheat oven to 375°F. Coat 2 large nonstick baking sheets with nonstick cooking spray.

2. Cut each halved wonton wrapper into 2 strips; place in single layer on prepared baking sheets.

3. Combine water, oil, paprika, cumin and mustard in small bowl; mix well. Brush oil mixture evenly onto wonton strips; sprinkle evenly with sesame seeds.

4. Bake 6 to 8 minutes or until lightly browned. Remove to wire rack; cool completely. Transfer to serving plate. *Makes 8 servings*

Nutrients per Serving: Calories: 75, Carbohydrate: 12g, Fiber: <1g, Protein: 2g, Fat: 2g, Saturated Fat: <1g, Cholesterol: 3mg, Sodium: 116mg

Helpful Hint

Sesame seeds are the seeds of a leafy green plant that is native to East Africa and Indonesia. These tiny round seeds are usually ivory colored, but brown, red and black sesame seeds are available. Sesame seeds, regardless of color, have a slightly sweet, nutty flavor. They are widely available packaged in supermarkets and are sold in bulk in specialty stores and ethnic markets. Because of their high oil content, they easily turn rancid and are best stored in the refrigerator where they will keep up to six months or they may be frozen up to a year.

Spiced Sesame Wonton Crisps

Spicy Shrimp Cocktail

2 tablespoons olive or vegetable oil
¼ cup finely chopped onion
1 tablespoon chopped green bell pepper
1 clove garlic, minced
1 can (8 ounces) CONTADINA® Tomato Sauce
1 tablespoon chopped pitted green olives, drained
¼ teaspoon red pepper flakes
1 pound cooked shrimp, chilled

1. Heat oil in small skillet. Add onion, bell pepper and garlic; sauté until vegetables are tender. Stir in tomato sauce, olives and red pepper flakes.

2. Bring to a boil; simmer, uncovered, for 5 minutes. Cover.

3. Chill thoroughly. Combine sauce with shrimp in small bowl.

Makes 6 servings

Prep Time: 6 minutes
Cook Time: 10 minutes

Nutrients per Serving: Calories: 129, Carbohydrate: 3g, Fiber: 1g, Protein: 17g, Fat: 6g, Saturated Fat: 1g, Cholesterol: 147mg, Sodium: 402mg

Red Hot Pepper Wings

28 chicken wing drumettes (2¼ to 3 pounds)
2 tablespoons olive oil
Salt and black pepper
2 tablespoons melted butter
1 teaspoon sugar
¼ to ½ cup hot pepper sauce

Brush chicken with oil; sprinkle with salt and pepper. Grill chicken on covered grill over medium KINGSFORD® Briquets about 20 minutes until juices run clear, turning every 5 minutes. Combine butter, sugar and pepper sauce in large bowl; add chicken and toss to coat. Serve hot or cold.

Makes 7 servings

Nutrients per Serving: Calories: 452, Carbohydrate: 4g, Fiber: 0g, Protein: 36g, Fat: 32g, Saturated Fat: 0g, Cholesterol: 124mg, Sodium: 31mg

Spicy Shrimp Cocktail

Szechuan Chicken Tenders

 2 tablespoons soy sauce
 1 tablespoon chili sauce
 1 tablespoon dry sherry
 2 cloves garlic, minced
 ¼ teaspoon red pepper flakes
16 chicken tenders (about 1 pound)
 1 tablespoon peanut oil
   Hot cooked rice

Combine soy sauce, chili sauce, sherry, garlic and red pepper in shallow dish. Add chicken; coat well.

Heat oil in large nonstick skillet over medium heat until hot. Add chicken; cook 6 minutes, turning once, until chicken is browned and no longer pink in center.

Serve chicken with rice, if desired. *Makes 4 servings*

Cook's Nook: If you can "take the heat," try adding a few Szechuan peppers to the dish. They are best if heated in the oven or over a low flame in a skillet for a few minutes beforehand.

Nutrients per Serving: Calories: 180, Carbohydrate: 3g, Fiber: <1g, Protein: 26g, Fat: 6g, Saturated Fat: 0g, Cholesterol: 69mg, Sodium: 625mg

Szechuan Chicken Tenders

Seafood Spread

1 package (8 ounces) cream cheese, softened
½ pound smoked whitefish, skinned, boned, flaked
2 tablespoons minced green onion
1 tablespoon plus 1 teaspoon chopped fresh dill
1 teaspoon lemon juice
¼ teaspoon black pepper

Beat cream cheese in medium bowl with electric mixer on medium speed until smooth. Add remaining ingredients, mixing until blended. Refrigerate until ready to serve. Serve with low carb rye bread slices. Garnish with lime wedges.   *Makes 1½ cups (12 servings)*

Prep time: 10 minutes plus refrigerating

Nutrients per Serving: Calories: 87, Carbohydrate: 1g, Fiber: <1g, Protein: 6g, Fat: 7g, Saturated Fat: 4g, Cholesterol: 27mg, Sodium: 249mg

Cherry-Peach Pops

⅓ cup peach nectar or apricot nectar
1 teaspoon unflavored gelatin
1 (15-ounce) can sliced peaches in light syrup, drained
1 (6- or 8-ounce) carton fat-free, sugar-free peach or cherry yogurt
1 (6- or 8-ounce) carton fat-free, sugar-free cherry yogurt

1. Combine nectar and unflavored gelatin in small saucepan; let stand 5 minutes. Heat and stir over low heat just until gelatin dissolves.

2. Combine nectar mixture, drained peaches and yogurts in food processor. Cover and process until smooth.

3. Pour into 7 (3-ounce) paper cups, filling each about ⅔ full. Place in freezer; freeze 1 hour. Insert wooden stick into center of each cup. Freeze at least 3 more hours.

4. Let stand at room temperature 10 minutes before serving. Tear away paper cups to serve.   *Makes 7 servings*

Nutrients per Serving: Calories: 52, Carbohydrate: 11g, Fiber: <1g, Protein: 2g, Fat: <1g, Saturated Fat: <1g, Cholesterol: 1mg, Sodium: 34mg

Seafood Spread

Baked Spinach Balls

2 cups sage and onion or herb-seasoned bread stuffing mix
2 tablespoons grated Parmesan cheese
1 small onion, chopped
1 clove garlic, minced
¼ teaspoon dried thyme leaves
¼ teaspoon black pepper
1 package (10 ounces) frozen chopped spinach, thawed and well
    drained
¼ cup fat-free reduced-sodium chicken broth
2 egg whites, beaten
    Dijon or honey mustard (optional)

1. Combine bread stuffing mix, cheese, onion, garlic, thyme and pepper
in medium bowl; mix well. Combine spinach, broth and egg whites in
separate medium bowl; mix well. Stir into bread cube mixture. Cover;
refrigerate 1 hour or until mixture is firm.

2. Preheat oven to 350°F. Shape mixture into 24 balls. Place on
ungreased baking sheet; bake 15 minutes or until spinach balls are
browned. Serve with mustard for dipping, if desired. Garnish, if desired.

Makes 12 servings

Nutrients per Serving: Calories: 52, Carbohydrate: 9g, Fiber: <1g,
Protein: 3g, Fat: 1g, Saturated Fat: <1g, Cholesterol: 1mg,
Sodium: 227mg

Baked Spinach Balls

Crab Canapés

 ⅔ cup fat-free cream cheese, softened
 2 teaspoons lemon juice
 1 teaspoon hot pepper sauce
 1 package (8 ounces) imitation crabmeat or lobster, flaked
 ⅓ cup chopped red bell pepper
 2 green onions with tops, sliced (about ¼ cup)
64 cucumber slices (about 2½ medium cucumbers cut ⅜ inch thick)
    or melba toast rounds

1. Combine cream cheese, lemon juice and hot pepper sauce in medium bowl; mix well. Stir in crabmeat, bell pepper and green onions; cover. Chill until ready to serve.

2. When ready to serve, spoon 1½ teaspoons crab mixture onto each cucumber slice. Place on serving plate; garnish with parsley, if desired.

Makes 16 servings

Nutrients per Serving: Calories: 31, Carbohydrate: 4g, Fiber: <1g, Protein: 4g, Fat: <1g, Saturated Fat: <1g, Cholesterol: 5mg, Sodium: 178mg

Helpful Hint

To allow flavors to blend, chill crab mixture at
least 1 hour before spreading onto cucumbers
or melba toast rounds.

Crab Canapés

Quick and Easy Stuffed Mushrooms

1 slice whole wheat bread
16 large mushrooms
1 clove garlic
½ cup sliced celery
½ cup sliced onion
1 teaspoon Worcestershire sauce
½ teaspoon marjoram leaves, crushed
⅛ teaspoon ground red pepper
Dash paprika

1. Tear bread into pieces; place in food processor. Process 30 seconds or until crumbs form. Transfer to small bowl; set aside.

2. Remove stems from mushrooms; reserve caps. Place mushroom stems, garlic, celery and onion in food processor. Process with on/off pulses until vegetables are finely chopped.

3. Preheat oven to 350°F. Coat nonstick skillet with cooking spray. Add mushroom mixture; cook and stir over medium heat 5 minutes or until onion is tender. Turn into bowl. Stir in bread crumbs, Worcestershire sauce, marjoram and ground red pepper.

4. Fill mushroom caps with mixture, pressing down firmly. Place filled caps in shallow baking pan about ½ inch apart. Spray lightly with nonstick cooking spray. Sprinkle with paprika. Bake 15 minutes or until hot.   *Makes 8 servings*

Note: Mushrooms may be stuffed up to 1 day ahead. Refrigerate filled mushroom caps, covered, until ready to serve. Bake in preheated 300°F oven 20 minutes or until hot.

Nutrients per Serving: Calories: 20, Carbohydrate: 4g, Fiber: 1g, Protein: 1g, Fat: <1g, Saturated Fat: <1g, Cholesterol: 0mg, Sodium: 29mg

Black Bean Bisque with Crab

3 cups low sodium chicken broth, defatted
1 jar (16 ounces) GUILTLESS GOURMET® Black Bean Dip (Spicy or Mild)
1 can (6 ounces) crabmeat, drained
2 tablespoons brandy (optional)
6 tablespoons low fat sour cream
   Chopped fresh chives (optional)

Microwave Directions
Combine broth and bean dip in 2-quart glass measure or microwave-safe casserole. Cover with vented plastic wrap or lid; microwave on HIGH (100% power) 6 minutes or until soup starts to bubble.

Stir in crabmeat and brandy, if desired; microwave on MEDIUM (50% power) 2 minutes or to desired serving temperature. To serve, ladle bisque into 8 individual ramekins or soup bowls, dividing evenly. Swirl 1 tablespoon sour cream into each serving. Garnish with chives, if desired.   *Makes 8 servings*

Stove Top Directions: Combine broth and bean dip in 2-quart saucepan; bring to a boil over medium heat. Stir in crabmeat and brandy, if desired; cook 2 minutes or to desired serving temperature. Serve as directed.

Nutrients per Serving: Calories: 104, Carbohydrate: 10g, Fiber: 2g, Protein: 11g, Fat: 1g, Saturated Fat: 1g, Cholesterol: 25mg, Sodium: 367mg

Get it on the Go

Chilled Shrimp in Chinese Mustard Sauce

- **1 cup water**
- **½ cup dry white wine**
- **2 tablespoons reduced-sodium soy sauce**
- **½ teaspoon Szechuan or black peppercorns**
- **1 pound raw large shrimp, peeled and deveined**
- **¼ cup prepared sweet and sour sauce**
- **2 teaspoons hot Chinese mustard**

1. Combine water, wine, soy sauce and peppercorns in medium saucepan. Bring to a boil over high heat. Add shrimp; reduce heat to medium. Cover and simmer 2 to 3 minutes or until shrimp are opaque. Drain well. Cover and refrigerate until chilled.

2. Combine sweet and sour sauce and mustard in small bowl; mix well. Serve as a dipping sauce for shrimp.   *Makes 6 servings*

Health Note: Shellfish, such as shrimp, is an excellent source of low-calorie, low-fat protein. It's also rich in the minerals iron, copper and zinc, yet low in sodium.

Nutrients per Serving: Calories: 92, Carbohydrate: 5g, Fiber: <1g, Protein: 13g, Fat: 1g, Saturated Fat: <1g, Cholesterol: 116mg, Sodium: 365mg

Chilled Shrimp in Chinese Mustard Sauce

Thai Lamb & Couscous Rolls

16 large napa or Chinese cabbage leaves, stems trimmed
2 tablespoons minced fresh ginger
1 teaspoon red pepper flakes
⅔ cup uncooked quick-cooking couscous
½ pound ground lean lamb
½ cup chopped green onions
3 cloves garlic, minced
¼ cup plus 2 tablespoons minced fresh cilantro or mint, divided
2 tablespoons reduced-sodium soy sauce
1 tablespoon lime juice
1 teaspoon dark sesame oil
1 cup plain nonfat yogurt

1. Place 4 cups water in medium saucepan; bring to a boil over high heat. Drop cabbage leaves into water; cook 30 seconds. Drain. Rinse under cold water until cool; pat dry with paper towels.

2. Place 1 cup water, ginger and red pepper in medium saucepan; bring to a boil over high heat. Stir in couscous; cover. Remove saucepan from heat; let stand 5 minutes.

3. Spray large saucepan with nonstick cooking spray; add lamb, onions and garlic. Cook and stir over medium-high heat 5 minutes or until lamb is no longer pink. Remove lamb from skillet; drain in colander.

4. Combine couscous, lamb mixture, ¼ cup cilantro, soy sauce, lime juice and oil in medium bowl. Spoon evenly down centers of cabbage leaves. Fold ends of cabbage leaves over filling; roll up. Combine yogurt and remaining 2 tablespoons cilantro in small bowl; spoon evenly over rolls. Serve warm. Garnish as desired.   *Makes 16 appetizers*

Nutrients per Serving: Calories: 53, Carbohydrate: 7g, Fiber: 1g, Protein: 4g, Fat: 1g, Saturated Fat: <1g, Cholesterol: 7mg, Sodium: 75mg

Thai Lamb & Couscous Rolls

Black Bean Quesadillas

Nonstick cooking spray
4 (8-inch) flour tortillas
¾ cup (3 ounces) shredded reduced-fat Monterey Jack or Cheddar
  cheese
½ cup canned black beans, rinsed and drained
2 green onions with tops, sliced
¼ cup minced fresh cilantro
½ teaspoon ground cumin
½ cup salsa
2 tablespoons plus 2 teaspoons fat-free sour cream

1. Preheat oven to 450°F. Spray large nonstick baking sheet with nonstick cooking spray. Place 2 tortillas on prepared baking sheet; sprinkle each with half the cheese.

2. Combine beans, green onions, cilantro and cumin in small bowl; mix lightly. Spoon bean mixture evenly over cheese; top with remaining tortillas. Coat tops with cooking spray.

3. Bake 10 to 12 minutes or until cheese is melted and tortillas are lightly browned. Cut into quarters; top each tortilla wedge with 1 tablespoon salsa and 1 teaspoon sour cream. Transfer to serving plate.

Makes 8 servings

Nutrients per Serving: Calories: 105, Carbohydrate: 13g, Fiber: 1g, Protein: 7g, Fat: 4g, Saturated Fat: 1g, Cholesterol: 8mg, Sodium: 259mg

Helpful Hint

Quesadillas are a versatile snack food. They can
be made up to a day ahead and refrigerated;
reheat them on a baking sheet in a 375°F oven
for 15 minutes.

Black Bean Quesadillas

Wild Wedges

    2 (8-inch) fat-free flour tortillas
      Nonstick cooking spray
    ⅓ cup shredded reduced-fat Cheddar cheese
    ⅓ cup chopped cooked chicken or turkey
    1 green onion, thinly sliced
    2 tablespoons mild, thick and chunky salsa

1. Heat large nonstick skillet over medium heat until hot.

2. Spray one side of one flour tortilla with cooking spray; place, sprayed side down, in skillet. Top with cheese, chicken, green onion and salsa. Place remaining tortilla over mixture; spray with cooking spray.

3. Cook 2 to 3 minutes per side or until golden brown and cheese is melted. Cut into 8 triangles.   *Makes 4 servings*

Variation: For bean quesadillas, omit the chicken and spread ⅓ cup canned fat-free refried beans over one of the tortillas.

Nutrients per Serving: Calories: 76, Carbohydrate: 8g, Fiber: 4g, Protein: 7g, Fat: 2g, Saturated Fat: 1g, Cholesterol: 14mg, Sodium: 282mg

Fast Guacamole and "Chips"

    2 ripe avocados
    ½ cup restaurant-style chunky salsa
    ¼ teaspoon hot pepper sauce (optional)
    ½ seedless cucumber, sliced into ⅛-inch rounds

1. Cut avocados in half; remove and discard pits. Scoop flesh into medium bowl. Mash with fork.

2. Add salsa and pepper sauce, if desired; mix well.

3. Transfer guacamole to serving bowl; surround with cucumber "chips".   *Makes 8 servings, about 1¾ cups*

Nutrients per Serving: Calories: 85, Carbohydrate: 5g, Fiber: 2g, Protein: 2g, Fat: 7g, Saturated Fat: 1g, Cholesterol: 0mg, Sodium: 120mg

Wild Wedges

Grilled Turkey Ham Quesadillas

Nonstick cooking spray
¼ cup salsa
4 (7-inch) flour tortillas
½ cup (2 ounces shredded reduced-sodium reduced-fat Monterey
  Jack cheese
¼ cup finely chopped turkey ham
1 can (4 ounces) diced green chilies, drained
  Additional salsa (optional)
  Fat-free sour cream (optional)

1. To prevent sticking, spray grid with cooking spray. Prepare coals for grilling.

2. Spread 1 tablespoon salsa onto each tortilla. Sprinkle cheese, turkey ham and chilies equally over half of each tortilla; fold over uncovered half to make "sandwich". Spray tops and bottoms of tortilla "sandwiches" with cooking spray.

3. Grill quesadillas on uncovered grill over medium coals 1½ minutes per side or until cheese is melted and tortillas are golden brown, turning once. Quarter each quesadilla and serve with additional salsa and nonfat sour cream, if desired.   *Makes 8 servings*

Nutrients per Serving: Calories: 66, Carbohydrate: 8g, Fiber: <1g, Protein: 4g, Fat: 2g, Saturated Fat: 1g, Cholesterol: 5mg, Sodium: 195mg

Rosemary Breadsticks

⅔ cup reduced-fat (2%) milk
¼ cup finely chopped fresh chives
2 teaspoons baking powder
1 teaspoon finely chopped fresh rosemary *or* ½ teaspoon dried
  rosemary
¾ teaspoon salt
½ teaspoon black pepper
¾ cup whole wheat flour
¾ cup all-purpose flour
  Nonstick cooking spray

1. Combine milk, chives, baking powder, rosemary, salt and pepper in large bowl; mix well. Stir in flours, ½ cup at a time, until blended. Turn onto floured surface and knead dough about 5 minutes or until smooth and elastic, adding more flour if dough is sticky. Let stand 30 minutes at room temperature.

2. Preheat oven to 375°F. Spray baking sheet with cooking spray. Divide dough into 12 balls, about 1¼ ounces each. Roll each ball into long thin rope; place on prepared baking sheet. Lightly spray breadsticks with cooking spray. Bake about 12 minutes or until bottoms are golden brown. Turn breadsticks over; bake about 10 minutes more or until golden brown.   *Makes 12 breadsticks*

Nutrients per Serving: Calories: 62, Carbohydrate: 12g, Fiber: 1g, Protein: 2g, Fat: 1g, Saturated Fat: <1g, Cholesterol: 1mg, Sodium: 196mg

Crab Cakes Canton

7 ounces thawed frozen cooked crabmeat or imitation crabmeat, drained and flaked
1½ cups fresh whole wheat bread crumbs (about 3 slices)
¼ cup thinly sliced green onions
1 clove garlic, minced
1 teaspoon minced fresh ginger
2 egg whites, lightly beaten
1 tablespoon teriyaki sauce
2 teaspoons vegetable oil, divided
Prepared sweet and sour sauce (optional)

Combine crabmeat, bread crumbs, onions, garlic and ginger in medium bowl; mix well. Add egg whites and teriyaki sauce; mix well. Shape into patties about ½ inch thick and 2 inches in diameter.*

Heat 1 teaspoon oil in large nonstick skillet over medium heat until hot. Add about half of crab cakes to skillet. Cook 2 minutes per side or until golden brown. Remove to warm serving plate; keep warm. Repeat with remaining 1 teaspoon oil and crab cakes. Serve with sweet and sour sauce, if desired.   *Makes 6 servings (12 cakes)*

*Crab cakes may be made ahead to this point; cover and refrigerate up to 24 hours before cooking.

Nutrients per Serving: Calories: 84, Carbohydrate: 6g, Fiber: <1g, Protein: 9g, Fat: 2g, Saturated Fat: <1g, Cholesterol: 18mg, Sodium: 480mg

Curly Lettuce Wrappers

4 green leaf lettuce leaves
¼ cup reduced-fat sour cream
4 turkey bacon slices, crisp-cooked and crumbled
½ cup (2 ounces) crumbled feta or blue cheese
8 ounces thinly sliced deli turkey breast
4 whole green onions
½ medium red or green bell pepper, thinly sliced
1 cup broccoli sprouts

1. Rinse lettuce leaves and pat dry.

2. Combine sour cream and bacon in small bowl. Spread ¼ of sour cream mixture evenly over center third of one lettuce leaf. Sprinkle 2 tablespoons cheese over sour cream. Top with 2 ounces turkey.

3. Cut off green portion of each green onion, reserving white onion bottoms for later use. Place green portion of 1 onion, ¼ of bell pepper slices and ¼ cup sprouts on top of turkey.

4. Fold right edge of lettuce over filling; fold bottom edge up over filling. Loosely roll up from folded right edge, leaving left edge of wrap open. Repeat with remaining ingredients.   *Makes 4 servings*

Travel Tip: Wrap individually in plastic wrap. Store in cooler with ice.

Nutrients per Serving: Calories: 155, Carbohydrate: 6g, Fiber: <1g, Protein: 17g, Fat: 7g, Saturated Fat: 4g, Cholesterol: 75mg, Sodium: 987mg

Curly Lettuce Wrapper

Mushrooms Rockefeller

18 large fresh button mushrooms (about 1 pound)
 2 slices bacon
 ¼ cup chopped onion
 1 package (10 ounces) frozen chopped spinach, thawed and
     squeezed dry
 1 tablespoon lemon juice
 1 teaspoon grated lemon peel
 ½ jar (2 ounces) chopped pimiento, drained
   Lemon slices and lemon balm for garnish

1. Lightly spray 13×9-inch baking dish with nonstick cooking spray.
Preheat oven to 375°F. Brush dirt from mushrooms; clean by wiping
mushrooms with damp paper towel. Pull entire stem out of each
mushroom cap.

2. Cut thin slice from base of each stem; discard. Chop stems.

3. Cook bacon in medium skillet over medium heat until crisp. Remove
bacon with tongs to paper towel; set aside. Add mushroom stems and
onion to hot drippings in skillet. Cook and stir until onion is soft. Add
spinach, lemon juice, lemon peel and pimiento; blend well. Stuff
mushroom caps with spinach mixture; place in single layer in prepared
baking dish. Crumble reserved bacon and sprinkle on top of
mushrooms. Bake 15 minutes or until heated through. Garnish, if
desired. Serve immediately.   *Makes 18 appetizers*

Nutrients per Serving: Calories: 17, Carbohydrate: 2g, Fiber: 1g,
Protein: 2g, Fat: <1g, Saturated Fat: <1g, Cholesterol: <1mg,
Sodium: 26mg

Helpful Hint

Button (or field) mushrooms are the most
common mushrooms grown and sold. They are
plump and dome-shaped with a smooth
texture and mild flavor. The color of button
mushrooms varies from white to pale tan.

Mushrooms Rockefeller

Late-night Nibble

Chocolate-Caramel S'Mores

12 chocolate wafer cookies or chocolate graham cracker squares
2 tablespoons fat-free caramel topping
6 large marshmallows

1. Prepare coals for grilling. Place 6 wafer cookies top down on plate. Spread 1 teaspoon caramel topping in center of each wafer to within about ¼ inch of edge.

2. Spear 1 to 2 marshmallows onto long wood-handled skewer.* Hold several inches above coals 3 to 5 minutes or until marshmallows are golden and very soft, turning slowly. Push 1 marshmallow off into center of caramel. Top with plain wafer. Repeat with remaining marshmallows and wafers.

Makes 6 servings

*If wood-handled skewers are unavailable, use oven mitt to protect hand from heat.

Tip: S'Mores, a favorite campfire treat, got their name because everyone who tasted them wanted "some more." In the unlikely event of leftover S'Mores, they can be reheated in the microwave at HIGH (100%) 15 to 30 seconds.

Nutrients per Serving: Calories: 72, Carbohydrate: 14g, Fiber: 0g, Protein: 1g, Fat: 2g, Saturated Fat: 1g, Cholesterol: 0mg, Sodium: 77mg

Chocolate-Caramel S'Mores

Roasted Garlic Spread with Three Cheeses

2 medium heads garlic
2 packages (8 ounces each) fat-free cream cheese, softened
1 package (3½ ounces) goat cheese
2 tablespoons (1 ounce) crumbled blue cheese
1 teaspoon dried thyme leaves

1. Preheat oven to 400°F. Cut tops off garlic heads to expose tops of cloves. Place garlic in small baking pan; bake 45 minutes or until garlic is very tender. Remove from pan; cool completely. Squeeze garlic into small bowl; mash with fork.

2. Beat cream cheese and goat cheese in small bowl until smooth; stir in blue cheese, garlic and thyme. Cover; refrigerate 3 hours or overnight. Spoon dip into serving bowl; serve with cucumbers, radishes, carrots, yellow bell peppers or crackers, if desired. Garnish with fresh thyme and red bell pepper strip, if desired. *Makes 21 servings*

Nutrients per Serving: Calories: 37, Carbohydrate: 2g, Fiber: <1g, Protein: 4g, Fat: 1g, Saturated Fat: <1g, Cholesterol: 9mg, Sodium: 157mg

Chocolate-Peanut Butter-Apple Treats

½ (8-ounce package) fat-free or reduced-fat cream cheese, softened
¼ cup reduced-fat chunky peanut butter
2 tablespoons mini chocolate chips
2 large apples

1. Combine cream cheese, peanut butter and chocolate chips in a small bowl; mix well.

2. Cut each apple into 12 wedges; discard stems and seeds. Spread about 1½ teaspoons of the mixture over each apple slice.
Makes 8 servings (4 apple wedges and 1½ teaspoons spread)

Nutrients per Serving: Calories: 101, Carbohydrate: 12g, Fiber: 2g, Protein: 4g, Fat: 4g, Saturated Fat: 1g, Cholesterol: 2mg, Sodium: 144mg

Roasted Garlic Spread with Three Cheeses

Savory Zucchini Stix

Nonstick olive oil cooking spray
3 tablespoons seasoned dry bread crumbs
2 tablespoons grated Parmesan cheese
1 egg white
1 teaspoon reduced-fat (2%) milk
2 small zucchini (about 4 ounces each), cut lengthwise into
    quarters
⅓ cup spaghetti sauce, warmed

1. Preheat oven to 400°F. Spray baking sheet with cooking spray; set aside.

2. Combine bread crumbs and Parmesan cheese in shallow dish. Combine egg white and milk in another shallow dish; beat with fork until well blended.

3. Dip each zucchini wedge first into crumb mixture, then into egg white mixture, letting excess drip back into dish. Roll again in crumb mixture to coat.

4. Place zucchini sticks on prepared baking sheet; coat well with cooking spray. Bake 15 to 18 minutes or until golden brown. Serve with spaghetti sauce.   *Makes 4 servings*

Nutrients per Serving: Calories: 69, Carbohydrate: 9g, Fiber: 1g, Protein: 4g, Fat: 2g, Saturated Fat: 1g, Cholesterol: 6mg, Sodium: 329mg

Helpful Hint

Refrigerate zucchini, unwashed, in a perforated
plastic bag for up to 5 days.

Savory Zucchini Stix

Taco Popcorn Olé

    9 **cups air-popped popcorn**
      Butter-flavored cooking spray
    1 **teaspoon chili powder**
    ½ **teaspoon salt**
    ½ **teaspoon garlic powder**
    ⅛ **teaspoon ground red pepper (optional)**

1. Preheat oven to 350°F. Line 15×10-inch jelly-roll pan with foil.

2. Place popcorn in single layer in prepared pan. Coat lightly with cooking spray.

3. Combine chili powder, salt, garlic powder and red pepper, if desired, in small bowl; sprinkle over popcorn. Mix lightly to coat evenly.

4. Bake 5 minutes or until hot, stirring gently after 3 minutes. Spread mixture in single layer on large sheet of foil to cool.

Makes 6 (1½-cup) servings

Tip: Store popcorn mixture in tightly covered container at room temperature up to 4 days.

Nutrients per Serving: Calories: 48, Carbohydrate: 10g, Fiber: 2g, Protein: 2g, Fat: 1g, Saturated Fat: <1g, Cholesterol: 0mg, Sodium: 199mg

Broiled SPAM™ Appetizers

    1 **(7-ounce) can SPAM® Classic, finely cubed**
    ⅓ **cup shredded Cheddar cheese**
    ¼ **cup finely chopped celery**
    ¼ **cup mayonnaise or salad dressing**
    1 **tablespoon chopped fresh parsley**
    ⅛ **teaspoon hot pepper sauce**
      Toast triangles, party rye slices or crackers

In medium bowl, combine all ingredients except toast. Spread mixture on toast triangles. Place on baking sheet. Broil 1 to 2 minutes or until cheese is melted.   *Makes 32 appetizers*

Nutrients per Serving: Calories: 20, Carbohydrate: 0g, Fiber: g, Protein: 1g, Fat: 2g, Saturated Fat: 0g, Cholesterol: 6mg, Sodium: 72mg

Taco Popcorn Olé

Easiest Three-Cheese Fondue

1 tablespoon margarine
¼ cup finely chopped onion
2 cloves garlic, minced
1 tablespoon all-purpose flour
¾ cup reduced-fat (2%) milk
2 cups (8 ounces) shredded mild or sharp Cheddar cheese
1 package (3 ounces) cream cheese, cut into cubes
½ cup (2 ounces) crumbled blue cheese
⅛ teaspoon ground red pepper
4 to 6 drops hot pepper sauce
Breadsticks and assorted fresh vegetables for dipping

1. Heat margarine in small saucepan over medium heat until melted. Add onion and garlic; cook and stir 2 to 3 minutes or until tender. Stir in flour; cook 2 minutes, stirring constantly.

2. Stir milk into saucepan; bring to a boil. Boil, stirring constantly, about 1 minute or until thickened. Reduce heat to low; add cheeses, stirring until melted. Stir in red pepper and pepper sauce. Pour fondue into serving dish. Serve with dippers.   *Makes 8 (3-tablespoon) servings*

Hint: For a special touch, sprinkle fondue with parsley and ground red pepper.

Lighten Up: To reduce the total fat, replace the Cheddar cheese and cream cheese with reduced-fat Cheddar and cream cheeses.

Prep and Cook Time: 20 minutes

Nutrients per Serving: Calories: 207, Carbohydrate: 3g, Fiber: <1g, Protein: 10g, Fat: 17g, Saturated Fat: 10g, Cholesterol: 48mg, Sodium: 334mg

Easiest Three-Cheese Fondue

The publisher would like to thank the companies and organizations listed below for the use of their recipes and photographs in this publication.

Colorado Potato Administrative Committee

Del Monte Corporation

Dole Food Company, Inc.

Egg Beaters®

Florida Department of Agriculture and Consumer Services, Bureau of Seafood and Aquaculture

Guiltless Gourmet®

Hormel Foods, LLC

The Kingsford Products Company

McIlhenny Company (TABASCO® brand Pepper Sauce)

Minnesota Cultivated Wild Rice Council

National Chicken Council / US Poultry & Egg Association

StarKist® Seafood Company

Uncle Ben's Inc.

Unilever Bestfoods North America

93

Index

METRIC CONVERSION CHART

VOLUME MEASUREMENTS (dry)

1/8 teaspoon = 0.5 mL
1/4 teaspoon = 1 mL
1/2 teaspoon = 2 mL
3/4 teaspoon = 4 mL
1 teaspoon = 5 mL
1 tablespoon = 15 mL
2 tablespoons = 30 mL
1/4 cup = 60 mL
1/3 cup = 75 mL
1/2 cup = 125 mL
2/3 cup = 150 mL
3/4 cup = 175 mL
1 cup = 250 mL
2 cups = 1 pint = 500 mL
3 cups = 750 mL
4 cups = 1 quart = 1 L

VOLUME MEASUREMENTS (fluid)

1 fluid ounce (2 tablespoons) = 30 mL
4 fluid ounces (1/2 cup) = 125 mL
8 fluid ounces (1 cup) = 250 mL
12 fluid ounces (1 1/2 cups) = 375 mL
16 fluid ounces (2 cups) = 500 mL

WEIGHTS (mass)

1/2 ounce = 15 g
1 ounce = 30 g
3 ounces = 90 g
4 ounces = 120 g
8 ounces = 225 g
10 ounces = 285 g
12 ounces = 360 g
16 ounces = 1 pound = 450 g

DIMENSIONS

1/16 inch = 2 mm
1/8 inch = 3 mm
1/4 inch = 6 mm
1/2 inch = 1.5 cm
3/4 inch = 2 cm
1 inch = 2.5 cm

OVEN TEMPERATURES

250°F = 120°C
275°F = 140°C
300°F = 150°C
325°F = 160°C
350°F = 180°C
375°F = 190°C
400°F = 200°C
425°F = 220°C
450°F = 230°C

BAKING PAN SIZES

Utensil	Size in Inches/Quarts	Metric Volume	Size in Centimeters
Baking or Cake Pan (square or rectangular)	8×8×2	2 L	20×20×5
	9×9×2	2.5 L	23×23×5
	12×8×2	3 L	30×20×5
	13×9×2	3.5 L	33×23×5
Loaf Pan	8×4×3	1.5 L	20×10×7
	9×5×3	2 L	23×13×7
Round Layer Cake Pan	8×1½	1.2 L	20×4
	9×1½	1.5 L	23×4
Pie Plate	8×1¼	750 mL	20×3
	9×1¼	1 L	23×3
Baking Dish or Casserole	1 quart	1 L	—
	1½ quart	1.5 L	—
	2 quart	2 L	—